FORTNITE

THE TOP 100

This edition published in Great Britain in 2019 by Dean,
an imprint of Egmont UK Limited
The Yellow Building, 1 Nicholas Road, London W11 4AN
www.egmont.co.uk

Written by Kevin Pettman
Designed by Design Button
Edited by Jane Riordan

ISBN 978 1 4052 9686 1
70820/001
Printed in Italy

ONLINE SAFETY FOR YOUNGER FANS

Spending time online is great fun! Here are a few simple rules to help younger
fans stay safe and keep the internet a great place to spend time.
For more advice and guidance, please see page 64 of this book.

- Never give out your real name – don't use it as your username.
- Never give out any of your personal details.
- Never tell anybody which school you go to or how old you are.
- Never tell anybody your password, except a parent or guardian.
- Be aware that you must be 13 or over to create an account on many sites. Always check
the site policy and ask a parent or guardian for permission before registering.
- Always tell a parent or guardian if something is worrying you.

Stay safe online. Any website addresses listed in this book are correct at the
time of going to print. However, Egmont is not responsible for content hosted by
third parties. Please be aware that online content can be subject to change and
websites can contain content that is unsuitable for children. We advise that
all children are supervised when using the internet.

Egmont takes its responsibility to the planet and its inhabitants very seriously.
We aim to use papers from well-managed forests run by responsible suppliers.

100% UNOFFICIAL

FORTNITE

THE TOP 100

CONTENTS

CALLING ALL FORTNITE FANS!

GET READY, GAMERS

- the Battle Royale top 100 of all time is about to be revealed! From wow-factor weapons to sick skins, epic explosives, incredible items and top team-play tips, this book's inventory is in overload. Drop in on map secrets, cool vehicles, survival strategies, brilliant builds ... it's a full-on *Fortnite* frenzy!

The ten sections each reveal a top 10 of the best bits to ever hit the game. Discover the most fearsome firearms, the legendary Limited Time Modes and crazy gadgets that give you the edge over your enemy. Each section also lets you pick out, record and describe your own fantasy *Fortnite* things. It's time to dream up deadly weapons, items, gear, builds, locations, phrases and stacks more that will help you secure a Victory Royale!

So join your squad and scramble from the Battle Bus - the clock's ticking on your ultimate *Fortnite* countdown!

TOP 10 ... SURVIVAL TIPS

Fortnite is all about sharpshooting, surviving the storm, reaching safe ground and constructing quick-fire builds. Check out these top 10 crucial strategies and secrets to help you last until the endgame!

1 AIM HIGH ✓

Get to the island quickly by skydiving – landing earlier than the others gives you the best chance of looting vital weapons and shields. Elimination at the beginning is totally not cool, so aim for a rooftop and raid the building immediately for chests. A high spot also lets you spy on who else is around.

2 SILENT ASSASSIN ✓

When you land, you're likely to be bunched with other players, especially if you're in a new or popular location. Harvesting mats (materials) is important, but bashing your pickaxe at trees and metal is loud and gives away your location, as does firing ammo – so stay silent and stealthy.

TOP TIP
Listen out for the twinkling sound that chests make. Follow the sound to bag some early loot and weapons.

3 RUSHING OUT ✓

Eliminating players is certainly key to reaching the late stages of a battle, but don't be tempted to rush out into the open and loot the load from a player you've just struck down. There could be sneaky snipers watching, ready to knock you the minute you appear in their sights!

4 MEGA MEDS ✓

Having a stash of healing items in your inventory can be the difference between staying in the game or suffering devastating damage. Medkits, bandages, chug jugs and slurp juices will all rejuvenate you. It's best to gulp a shield potion as soon as you collect one to restore between 25 to 50 shield points. Don't forget, you can stack plenty of these, too.

5 WEAPON RANGE ✓

Keep a variety of weapons at your fingertips so that you can react to any shoot-out situation. Ditch low-powered pistols and hand cannons for shotguns, which are ace in close-range combat. Sniper rifles let you take shots safely from distance and assault rifles are awesome in medium- to long-range battles. There's more on weapons on page 12.

6 WOOD RULES ✓

Metal and stone are much stronger building resources, but keep your wood harvest count high at all times. Wood is the quickest material to build with and throwing up a protective base or shield from this source could keep you alive and able to respond to the enemy in less time. Try to keep all three mats above 300 as you progress in a game.

TOP TIP
Smashing wooden pallets is the most effective way to farm wood. They break quickly and reward you with a mega bunch of resources!

STORM CHASER

It's a simple rule, but get caught in the storm and you'll suffer severe damage and eventually be eliminated. You could stay on the edge, moving in to pick off players on the outskirts, or always position yourself well inside the storm's safe zone. Use vehicles or deploy your glider as this is faster than running across the map to safety.

TOP TIP
In the final phase, remember that the storm will punish you with ten damage per second. Keep an eye on your health as well as the storm circle's movement!

GUN CONTROL

Don't be trigger-happy and continuously fire bullets. For a start, you'll use up ammo at a much faster rate than needed. Holding the fire button increases your gun's 'spray', which means your accuracy suffers. Use short, sharp bursts and if you're experienced in hitting a moving target, jump up and down to make yourself a difficult target if your enemy retaliates.

9 SWITCH IT UP

Have a good combo of weapons, such as a shotgun and rifle, next to each other in your inventory. You'll then be able to toggle quickly between them to help finish off an opponent. Tactical shotguns can take six seconds to reload, so switch to another weapon after that to avoid the lengthy – and potentially lethal – reload delay.

10 KILL COUNT

Don't worry about this! The aim of Battle Royale is to be the last person standing, not the one who eliminates the most players on the island. You'll need at least one kill to claim a Victory Royale, but be smart and tactical. Only put yourself in danger and pull the trigger when needed.

TOP TIP
Headshots are the best way to take an enemy down. If you have time, line up this shot first to cause maximum damage, followed with a tap to the body to get the job done if needed.

FORTNITE FILE

MY FAVE *FORTNITE* SURVIVAL TIP IS:

MY BEST SURVIVAL TIP IN SQUADS IS:

SURVIVAL TIPS I'VE USED ...

☐ **LANDING QUICKLY**

☐ **STAYING ON THE EDGE OF THE STORM**

☐ **LANDING ON HIGH GROUND**

☐ **ORGANISING MY WEAPONS**

☐ **PERFECTING LONG-RANGE SNIPES**

☐ **HEALING AT THE RIGHT TIME**

☐ **CONTROLLING CLOSE-QUARTERS COMBAT**

MY TOP 3 SURVIVAL RECORDS:

	DATE OF BATTLE	SURVIVAL STRATEGY
1		
2		
3		

TOP 10 ... WEAPONS

Gameplay strategies and survival tips mean nothing if you don't have the best weapons at your fingertips! Check out our top ten of all time and what they can deliver for you on the island ...

SCAR ASSAULT RIFLE

Whether you're a beginner or a pro, most gamers reckon the SCAR assault rifles are the best all-round weapons. The Legendary version has a damage per second (DPS) value of 198, with structural damage of 36. The massive mag size means you can keep firing at mid-range and reload time is a manageable 2.1 seconds. Not easy to locate, but bag it if you can!

HEAVY SNIPER RIFLE

When it dropped in Season 5, the heavy sniper rifle became the most powerful weapon on the island! With a damage value of 157, it packs enough power to one-shot most opponents. Its 1,100 structural damage will take down forts with no worries. The heavy only fires a single shot and has a long reload time, so users need to be on target and wise with the weapon!

PUMP SHOTGUN

Is the pump better than the tactical shotgun? Well, the pump reloads quicker and at close-range its pellets will be tight to focus damage to an area on your opponent. It's an awesome firearm to have in one of your slots and does the business from Uncommon right up to Legendary – although we'd always take the orange monster, obvs!

ROCKET LAUNCHER

Often called the RPG (rocket-propelled grenade), this beauty is a beast of a weapon! Its primary use should be to take out bases and send enemy squads scurrying out into the open. Try to land the rocket inside a structure or base, rather than just against an outside wall, as you'll damage the building and potentially your opponents, too. It takes over three seconds to reload, which is a pain, so patience is needed with this one.

TOP TIP
Rocket launchers can be blocked. If you hear or see one on its way to you, quickly construct a wall and take shelter.

COMPACT SMG

This submachine gun may look a little weird (like a cross between a stapler and an assault rifle!) but it's definitely not to be laughed at in combat. Face one of these in close-quarters fighting and you could be eliminated in no time. It has a good fire rate and takes 40 light ammo per mag, which will keep you busy and blasting for long enough to knock opponents.

MINIGUN

Okay, so there are other weapons that cause more damage. But for sheer scary looks and cool sounds, the minigun shouldn't be dropped from your slots! This rotating auto-firing gun never needs to be reloaded, however, it will overheat and stop if the trigger's pushed for six seconds without pause. Fire in fearsome bursts to strike down other squads.

TOP TIP
The minigun has a short startup delay, so use cover from your teammates as the machine whirls into frenzied action!

BOLT-ACTION SNIPER RIFLE

7

Another sniper in this top ten? Yep – the 'boltie' is an unbelievable asset when you want to strike from distance! Both the Epic and Rare versions cause damage of over 100 and if you're an expert sniper, you'll fancy your chances of making impact after aiming down the scope. The snag is you can only operate the bolt-action in Playground and Creative.

TOP TIP
Sniper rifles are not 'hitscan', meaning the bullets take a short time to travel to their target and also drop slightly. Factor this in when sniping.

REMOTE EXPLOSIVES

8

Vaulted and dropped into Creative mode back in Season 7, you'll have a 'blast' bringing remote explosives into gameplay! Kicking out 400 damage to anyone caught in its wake, it works by being lobbed and attached to something and then shot at to activate. Beware though, as others can detonate remotes and potentially knock you down!

9

GRENADE LAUNCHER

Not easy to loot, but if you can find a grenade launcher, keep it ready for the endgame. It takes skill to deliver the rocket safely into the building or zone you're targeting, but master this and you'll be a key player for your team. Legendary launchers zap buildings with over 400 damage!

TOP TIP
Practise using the 'nade launcher in Playground mode so that you can perfect the technique of looping and landing rockets right into an enemy base.

10

THERMAL SCOPED ASSAULT RIFLE

Scoped weapons are epic at spotting targets from afar and lining up a lethal surprise hit. The thermal's secret skill is that it can also detect enemy heat signatures, chests and supply drops by zooming in. It's a really fab upgrade to the regular scoped assault, so keep it well topped up with medium ammo and be sure to learn how to boss this semi-auto superstar!

FORTNITE FILE

MY FAVE CURRENT *FORTNITE* WEAPON IS:

MY FAVE *FORTNITE* WEAPON COMBINATION IS:

MY FAVE VAULTED *FORTNITE* WEAPON IS:

MY TOP SHOOTING TIP IS:

MY DREAM *FORTNITE* WEAPON WOULD BE CALLED:

ITS STATS WOULD BE ...

DPS: **FIRE RATE:**   **MAG SIZE:**   **RELOAD TIME:**

DRAW A PICTURE BELOW OF THE DEADLY WEAPON YOU'D DESIGN!

TOP 10 ... BUILDS

From basic protection structures to incredible Creative constructions, these pages are packed with vital Battle Royale buildings and tips! Get your materials ready and master what it takes to build with the best ...

1 FUNNEL FORT

A funnel can easily be added to the top of a medium or tall tower building. It uses outwards ramps to create a cone-like shape, which lets you creep up to the edge for shooting and retreat back down if you're under attack.

TOP TIP
Make sure your control configurations are set to Builder Pro - this helps you construct quickly and efficiently.

2 HEALING ROOM

After a tense battle, knock up a basic box-like healing room to give you and your team time to use meds and restore health. If you have time, add a roof to protect from RPGs and a door for a quick exit!

3 RAMP RUSHING

Trying to eliminate an opponent who is at the top of a tall tower can be tricky. Don't climb up inside – create ramps up to them and pick them off. Building double ramps gives you more protection from bullets and can prevent you from falling to your death!

SNIPER TOWER

In Duos, construct a six-walled base that's between two to four levels high. Place opposite ramps leading up to the top edge, where you can both spy on your opponents and spray bullets down below!

PYRAMID

Placing pyramid roofs on buildings or inside a building is clever. For example, a pyramid beside an internal window lets you crawl around near the window and peek out. Also try editing and removing a corner of a roof pyramid to make a protective sniper's perch!

PANIC BUILD

Every player needs to know how to knock up a simple protective wall in a split second when under attack! You can even build a long screen of panic walls as you take cover.

TOP TIP
It's tricky, but placing a pyramid above your enemy while they are building ramps can block them off and slow them down.

TOWER BASE

Taking the high ground makes you a greater threat and increases the chances of collecting kills. A trusty 1x1 tower base, with internal ramps and a closed pointed roof, is simple but essential in many combat situations. Edit in a window to snipe from.

PLATFORMS

Platforms are ledges, paths or long horizontal walkways built outwards from buildings. They can be added to ramps and used to link two forts together. Platforms can also help you move across the map or from mountains just like a bridge would.

LOOMING LLAMA

The craziest creation to ever reach The Block is probably the Looming Llama. It took over 60 hours to build and needed more mats than anything that ever existed before, it's like a never-ending mechanical nightmare! Oh, and it looks a bit like a robot llama - hence the name!

TRAP ROOM

Using trap items, knock up a spiky scene like the one below, then lure the enemy in to finish them off! Traps are an epic way to knock your opponent. If they fall into a trap room from a high point, the dangerous walls could spring into action and eliminate them. They'll be trapped and zapped!

FORTNITE FILE

MY FAVE THING TO BUILD IN BATTLE ROYALE IS:

THE MOST ESSENTIAL THING TO BUILD IS:

THE MOST DIFFICULT THING TO BUILD IS:

MY TOP 3 BUILDING TIPS ARE:

1

2

3

DRAW YOUR ULTIMATE FORNITE BASE BELOW!

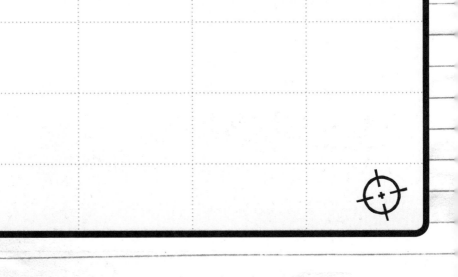

TOP 10 ... ITEMS

To be a battleground boss, you've got to know how to locate, use and master your items. From healing to explosives, traps and disguises, items are essential if your squad's shooting for success in the final phase. Discover the top ten and the tactics to take you to victory!

1 CHUG JUG

You can only carry one at a time, but a chug jug can be the difference between survival and elimination! This Legendary healing item boosts both health and shields to the max, but it does take 15 seconds to use, so take cover before downing the contents. Neck it after a frantic fight and you'll be good to go gunning again!

TOP TIP
In Squads and Duos, chug jugs can be shared with your team. Give a mate a vital lift so that you're all in top shape for combat.

2 BUSH

Take cover and creep up on the enemy with this epic consumable item! It looks simple, but search out a bush in chests and supply drops and it'll disguise you and allow you to move unsighted. It's always really fun being a bush, but watch out! Any damage you suffer will wipe it out and leave you out in the open and exposed. Eek!

3

MOUNTED TURRET

Classed as a trap item, the mega mounted turret first dropped in a Season 6 update and gives you unlimited ammo. It can only be placed on floors and will overheat if you're too trigger-happy, but get behind one of these Legendary items and the enemy will soon scatter! Keep your eyes peeled for it in drops, floor loots and llamas.

4

IMPULSE GRENADE

Should a top-level player ever act on impulse in Battle Royale? Well, if you have the impulse grenade, you'll definitely create some crazy scenes! Lob this rare item into a bunch of players and its impact will launch them into the air and totally disrupt their game. It doesn't deal damage but it could certainly give you the edge in a firefight.

TOP TIP
Unleash this grenade in Squads play, when players are likely to be bunched up, for maximum mayhem!

5

CLINGER GRENADE

Another grenade item, but this one dishes out a deadly 100 damage to players and is a real game-changer! The clinger sticks to an opponent or building and after 2.5 seconds it'll explode and cause carnage. Another bonus is that you can carry ten of these bad boys at once – that's a seriously sticky situation for the enemy!

6

LAUNCH PAD

Launch pads have been in Battle Royale since Season 1, but they are still an ultra-effective item in tactical battles. To deploy it quickly, lay a flat floor tile and then the pad and you can use it to bounce into the air and zoom to safety using your glider. It's most effective used at height as you'll get much more distance and speed high in the skies.

TOP TIP
Remember that the launch pad can be used by anyone. It can't be picked up, but can be smashed like other traps.

STINK BOMB

Do you fancy inflicting damage and having a laugh at the enemy's expense? It's time to 'think stink' then! Roll out a stink bomb and its murky cloud will deal five damage every 0.5 seconds for up to nine seconds. That certainly 'smells' trouble for any squad trying to take you down!

TOP TIP
The stink bomb thrower can also suffer in its smelly cloud, so don't chuck one and then enter its area.

CHILLER TRAP

Even though these were vaulted in Season 7, you can still have some freezin' fun with them in Playground mode. A chiller trap tile will send you or your enemy skidding like crazy, at much faster speeds than normal running. It's effective when you're being chased as it could cause the pursuer to fall off structures or high ground, leaving you time to chill out!

COZY CAMPFIRE

If the coast is clear and you're not under attack, a cozy campfire is a top way to restore your squad for the final phase. Rest close to it and the fire will increase health by up to 50 points at a rate of 2 points per second. It's not quick but will be a tactical team boost!

TOP TIP
Create a simple 1x1 defence from wood and place the campfire behind it. That way you'll have protection from any sneaky enemy raids.

BOUNCER

Hop over to Playground or Creative and have stacks of fun with the bouncer trap! Place it on the floor or walls, make contact and enjoy flying back off it for a quick escape or to make a surprise approach on your target. You won't receive any fall damage either.

FORTNITE FILE

MY FAVE *FORTNITE* ITEM IS:

MY ULTIMATE ITEM WOULD BE:

DRAW WHAT YOUR ITEM WOULD LOOK LIKE BELOW:

TOP 10 ... TRANSPORTS

Sometimes you don't want to run or walk across the island – cruising in vehicles and transport gadgets is way more fun! Take a look at our top ten transports to have ever dropped on the map, then dream up your own epic wheels and machines!

THE BALLER

Season 8 sprang a surprise with the release of the baller – a crazy vehicle that will help you outfox other gamers! It's a single-seat moving ball that protects the driver, fires a grappler to pull and swing you around terrain and has a helpful boost option. Players should keep their eyes peeled for one around expedition outposts and pirate camp loot stashes.

SHOPPING CART

Shopping carts, the very first vehicle to drop, handle one player pushing it or, in Duos, take a second passenger in the cart who can shoot at targets. Carts aren't super quick ... unless players speed down a hillside! Sadly they were vaulted in Season 8, so are limited to Playground and Creative.

TOP TIP
Unlike other early vehicles, such as ATKs and quadcrashers, shopping carts do not have brakes. Ride 'em with care!

3

X-4 STORMWING

Transport finally took to the skies in the icy update of Season 7! In one of the most thrilling vehicles to feature in *Fortnite*, up to five players (four wing-riders and a pilot) could speed away on the stormwing and blast away with the mounted machine gun. It's not all plane sailing though – get shot down and you'll suffer fall damage.

4

GLIDER

No top ten transport countdown is complete without the glorious glider! Along with the pickaxe, it's an essential bit of kit for gameplay and will deploy as you drop from the bus. Gliders can also be redeployed during a game when you're at height to help you move from the storm or escape an attack. V-bucks and Battle Passes will unlock fresh new glider designs.

TOP TIP
Watch out for players falling with an umbrella – this means they have a Victory Royale under their belt and will be tough to beat!

QUADCRASHER

Smashing, bashing, breaking – the quadcrasher does it all! Drive in Solo or have your Duos buddy stand on the back with their weapon ready. This hardcore four-wheeled bike builds boost as you move, which can be unleashed to help smash through most surroundings. It has been vaulted, but be revvin' and ready for when it returns to the main map!

DRIFTBOARD

With a speed advantage over the cart and ATK, plus much more mobility and tricks, the driftboard is fun and helpful in Battle Royale. It'll skim over snow, fields and water and slow down slightly as you aim a weapon at the enemy. Become a board pro and you'll have a brand new attack tactic!

TOP TIP
You can shoot, harvest and revive on the driftboard, but you can't build. If you come under fire, you'll need to hop off it to construct shelter.

7

ALL TERRAIN KART

Better known as the ATK, four team members can jump into this cool kart and cause havoc on the move. Pull out some awesome drifts and if you set off red sparks as you cruise, your speed boost will kick in. Watch out, though, as the ATK is a noisy machine and nearby enemies will be alerted as you rock on down the road!

8

SLIPSTREAMS

Okay, so they're not technically a machine or mechanical device. But when slipstreams, basically huge wind portals, were released in Season 9, transporting around the island became a whole lot easier! Enter a slipstream and it'll lift you up and fly you off to a different location in no time. It's the way to travel in the future, dudes!

9

PIRATE CANNON

When the island had a pirate party makeover in Season 8, one of the coolest updates was the powerful pirate cannons! Players could hide inside the weapon and be shot out by a teammate, or launch themselves to travel a huge distance across the map. Not strictly a vehicle or transport, but a guaranteed blast of fun!

10

BATTLE BUS

Finally, the battle bus is the most famous vehicle in the *Fortnite* universe – without it there just wouldn't be any Battle Royale action! Sometimes it is decorated and jazzed up to celebrate a *Fortnite* landmark. The bus will always be the starting point of a game and the spot where tactics are prepared ahead of skydiving and gliding. You gotta love the 'BB'!

FORTNITE FILE

MY FAVE CURRENT *FORTNITE* TRANSPORT IS:

MY FAVE VAULTED TRANSPORT IS:

MY ULTIMATE VEHICLE WOULD HAVE:

4 WHEELS: ☐   **2 WHEELS:** ☐   **FLYING POWERS:** ☐

BUILT-IN WEAPONS: ☐   **SUPER SPEED:** ☐

DRAW AND DESIGN YOUR DREAM *FORTNITE* VEHICLE BELOW ...

TOP 10 ... LIMITED TIME MODES

Pick your weapons, top up your health and get ready for some legendary LTM action! These special events send *Fortnite* fans wild and are full of mind-blowing new items, rules, features and team tactics. Drop in on this terrific top ten list, then create your own LTM on the final page ...

FLOOR IS LAVA

One of the 'hottest' updates ever on the island – gamers must reach the high ground and keep off the boiling lava! The volcano spews hot liquid, which gradually rises and means players need to build upwards to stay safe in this LTM nightmare. Put your feet on the lava and you'll take damage and be bounced into the air!

TOP TIP
In Floor is Lava, gamers get a small amount of mats every second so that they can keep building. You need quick construction skills here!

50 VS 50

Did you know that 50 vs 50 was the first LTM? Until its original launch in December 2017, all *Fortnite* battles were solo affairs, as 100 players took part in a free-for-all. The 50 frenzy is still a mega LTM, packed with frantic fun, teamwork tests and the need for sharp reactions and shooting. Players dropping from two different buses is pretty crazy, hey?!

FORTNITEMARES

At Halloween, *Fortnite* fans love to scare themselves silly with this spooky LTM! There is all sorts going on around the map, with gargoyles, monsters crawling out, and devastating weapons, such as the crossbow, making a special appearance. If you're feeling brave enough and you dare to come out and play, there are scary sights around every corner!

SOLID GOLD

Imagine an event where all the weapons to loot and discover are Legendary? Well, in Solid Gold, that's exactly what happens! This lethal LTM Squads mode has appeared several times in *Fortnite*, and you'll get extra mats when you farm resources in a bid to keep you alive against Legendary ARs and miniguns!

TOP TIP
There's often a higher drop rate of chug jugs and slurp juices, so make the most of these to keep your health maxed up.

5

HIGH EXPLOSIVES

Take cover ... it's a BOOM bonanza on the island! Most *Fortnite* fans will be aware of the High Explosives LTM, where players battle it out with only a dangerous arsenal of RPGs, grenades, grenade launchers and guided missiles. Drops and chests are stuffed with explosives and whether it's Solo or Squads, you need to be bang on with your targeting!

6

TEAM RUMBLE

Check out these crazy LTM rules: teams of 20 scrap it out with the goal of being the first to reach 100 kills! Sounds savage, doesn't it? It is, and it is totally addictive and frantic. The big deal is that gamers respawn five seconds after elimination, meaning tactics, sneaky sniping and hiding can fly out of the window. It's basically totally nuts!

TOP TIP
Respawning gives you random resources and ammo. Keep an eye on your inventory, don't waste bullets or give other teams an easy kill as they target the magical 100!

7

ONE SHOT

Are you a super sniper? The One Shot event is perfect for you – the only weapons are rifles, every player's health is set to 50 and there are no shields. Pick up something red-hot, like the hunting rifle, and land a one-shot on the opposition to move yourself towards victory. Healing is usually restricted to just bandages though, so don't leave yourself exposed on the battlefield.

8

DISCO DOMINATION

Guys, get your groove on if you want to grab a Victory Royale for your team! The Disco Domination LTM is pretty strange, but basically teams must capture dance floors around the map, then dance to be the first to raise a glittering disco ball up from the floor. Obviously the other team will try to shoot you down as you strut and boogie. Really weird!

9

GROUND GAME

This testing Limited Time Mode really separates the pros from the beginners! Resources are hugely restricted, limited to around 30 wood and 20 stone and metal, with ammo levels nerfed, too. It means that players must find natural cover and can't build huge forts and ramps. You really need to make every move – and bullet – count!

10

UNVAULTED

There's no way there could be a top ten LTM countdown without Unvaulted! Just as its name suggests, this mode features all the amazing weapons, items and vehicles that have been vaulted in the game. Excited? For sure. Get your hands on the bolt-action sniper, drum gun, tactical SMG, shockwave grenade, remote explosives and so much more. Sick *Fortnite* scenes!

FORTNITE FILE

MY FAVE CURRENT LTM IS:

MY FAVE LTM OF ALL TIME IS:

THE BEST LTMS HAVE:

SMALL TEAMS: ☐ **LARGE TEAMS:** ☐ **OP WEAPONS:** ☐

VARIETY OF WEAPONS: ☐ **DIFFERENT MAP FEATURES:** ☐

BELOW, YOU CAN DRAW A *FORTNITE* POSTER THAT ADVERTISES YOUR OWN LTM

EVENT – INCLUDE KEY WORDS, PICTURES AND A MEMORABLE NAME FOR IT!

TOP 10 ... AREAS

The map is always changing, but we all have our favourite *Fortnite* places, zones and secret spots. Discover ten of the best areas on the island and dream up your own lethal location on page 45!

NEO TOWERS

Previously known as Tilted Towers, this area has seen plenty of changes over the seasons – craters, the Cube, snow and ice have all impacted on it! In Season 9, it returned with a futuristic, neon-coloured theme and became known as Neo Tilted. It will feel familiar to most gamers roaming its streets, but it's still a high-risk environment with lots of sniper spots and hiding places for the enemy.

TOP TIP
Squads regularly avoid Neo Tilted because it can be hard to cover each other's backs among the crowded streets and buildings.

HIGH WATCHTOWER

If you leave the bus at the right time and glide into the eastern location of Lonely Lodge, try to land on top of the watchtower. You should crack open a few chests here, get geared up and be able to defend yourself against any opposition coming up the stairs. Redeploy your glider and zoom off from the top if you need to!

PIRATE SHIP

Not a secret sight at all – it's impossible to miss – the huge pirate ship that appeared in Season 8's Lazy Lagoon is stuffed with treasure. Four or five chests can be looted around its decks, with the added bonus of the pirate cannon blasters – shoot yourself from them for a crazy way to break buildings and enemies!

FORK KNIFE

The creatives behind *Fortnite* like to have a laugh placing 'fork knife' stuff around the map, like the food truck back in Season 6. In 2019, an update near Fatal Fields added ground trenches shaped like a fork and knife. LOL! But if you were an early visitor here, you could have been eliminated as a glitch killed players who dropped onto the edge of the knife. Unlucky!

TOP TIP
If you're heading into the farming fest that is Fatal Fields, don't forget to look behind haystacks for hidden chests.

RACE TRACKS

5

We couldn't decide between the racetrack near Happy Hamlet or the one in Paradise Palms ... so we choose both! You can use the baller and grappler to complete a slippery circuit in HH, or jump in an ATK and record a hot lap in the desert racecourse. These won't help you bag a Victory Royale, but will put a big smile on your *Fortnite* face!

POLAR PEAK CASTLE

6

The snowy scenes of Polar Peak instantly became a smash hit with gamers in Season 7. Underneath the snow was a cool castle and tower buildings and, as it gradually melted, *Fortnite* fans discovered secret tunnels, entrances and fortress buildings. The map changed before your eyes and even lead to the Ice King appearing later on!

TOP TIP
If you haven't visited an area for a few days or weeks, ask your squad – or other *Fortnite* friends – if there are any map updates or changes you need to be aware of!

RETAIL ROW

If the bullet bonanzas of Tilted and Paradise Palms are too much for you, try dropping in on Retail Row instead. It's a safer zone for gamers with less experience but is still decked out with restaurants and stores that house useful loot. Retail Row often gets busier as the game moves on, so do your stuff and get outta there!

TOP TIP
Close doors behind you when you enter a building. An open door may alert gamers that you're inside and ready to be ambushed!

EXPEDITION OUTPOSTS

Some weekly challenges involve visiting expedition outposts, which are big, red bases that are usually easy to spot. These outposts often spawn chests and may have cool new things near them, like ziplines and ballers in the past. Take a sneaky look around them when you can and collect gear that'll help you reach the exciting latter stages!

THE BLOCK

9

We hear you – The Block isn't strictly an area on the regular *Fortnite* map, but it's definitely a place to check out! When normal gamers, just like you, build a truly awesome place, it can be shared with the game makers. If selected, it will be placed in The Block for millions around the world to try out. A mind-blowing update, for sure!

TOP TIP
Keep sharpening your skills and builds in the Creative section. It's the only way you can dream of joining The Block one day!

MOUNTAINS

10

They are tricky to reach, often needing lots of mats or a flying or propulsion device, but being perched out with your squad on a mountain or hilltop can be sooo rewarding! From here, scoped rifles can do amazing damage to unsuspecting opposition down below. The west of the island has a good range of high spots, especially around Pleasant Park.

FORTNITE FILE

MY FAVE *FORTNITE* PLACE IS:

MY FAVE PLACE THAT'S BEEN REMOVED IS:

THE BEST LOCATIONS HAVE:

LOTS OF BUILDINGS: ☐   **CHESTS:** ☐   **SECRET PLACES:** ☐

MATS TO HARVEST: ☐   **SNIPER SPOTS:** ☐

FANCY CREATING YOUR OWN *FORTNITE* LOCATION? SCRIBBLE AN IMAGE OF WHAT IT

WOULD LOOK LIKE HERE ...

TOP 10 ... EPIC THINGS

This section is loaded with the random, one-off or special things that make *Fortnite* the most epic battle game ever. From weapons to items, cosmetics and crazy challenges, check out the sick stuff we reckon needs your attention!

INFINITY BLADE

Without doubt, this is the most epic thing ever to happen in *Fortnite*! Appearing at Christmas 2018, the person who pulled the mythical blade from its stone was granted max health and shield, could leap around like a giant and strike opponents down with one slash. The infinity blade was so powerful that it was vaulted a few days later, but did return to Creative. Totally, totally savage!

SHADOW STONES

Instant invisibility is what these beauties brought to *Fortnite* in Season 6. They could be used to make yourself disappear in the enemy's eyes while you stood still, but if you moved while under their effect you left a misty trail. Kick in the 'phase' option and you'd be propelled through objects and walls. Mystical, magical ... and mega handy!

3

PORT-A-FORT

Gamers grumbled when the port-a-fort was vaulted in Season 7, but they'll never forget what a mighty combat tool it was! When this rare item was detonated, it instantly created a three-storey fortress with a sniper's funnel at the top. It even came with bounce tyres to leap you into it. It was a proper game-changer.

TOP TIP
Drop the port-a-fort as close to you as possible so that you don't have to travel across open ground during combat to reach it.

4

PETS

They serve no purpose other than fancy back bling, but who doesn't want a seriously cute companion? Dogs, dragons, foxes and chameleons are among the cast of mini characters that can join you. They also react to what's happening in the game – even in Solo you won't be alone and will always have a likeable friend. Robo pets first appeared in Season 9 with Kyo – the coolest creature around!

47

ZIPLINES

Things like vehicles, launch pads and gliders are not the only way to quickly move around the map – ziplines will speed you to a new area as well. Attach yourself and hang in as you slide away from danger or drop in on a chest-tastic spot. It's much faster than walking, so get to know where they are and use them to escape the storm, too.

TOP TIP
Be careful – dangling on a zip will make you stand out to the enemy. If you detach at height you'll suffer fall damage.

RIFT-TO-GO

Rifts caused all sorts of riots in Season 5, allowing players to enter them and instantly skydive or glide to spring a surprise. A rift-to-go item can be unleashed when you want, either when you're on foot or in a vehicle, and will propel you to the skies and bamboozle other gamers. Very useful!

ESPORTS

When a $100 million prize pool for *Fortnite* eSports was revealed, everyone got excited. eSports are gaming competitions, either for players at home or at a venue, with successful players winning cash prizes. Usually you need to be 13 or older and have guardian permission, with events like *Fortnite* World Cup, Skirmish and Winter Royale attracting thousands of entries.

WRAPS

Just before Christmas, Epic put wraps into *Fortnite*. Were they wrapping presents when they thought of it? Wraps are available from the item shop or as Battle Pass rewards. Choose one and your weapons and vehicle will automatically take on a new appearance and texture. It's a cool cosmetic – arctic camo, durr burger, tiger and carbon gold are our faves!

TOP TIP
The pink 'cuddle hearts' wrap was available for free, as long as you could get a special code to bag it from the item shop. Look out for future coded freebies.

CRAZY CHALLENGE

Fortnite has weekly challenges to complete, which are fun, but try creating your own crazy challenges. It's by far one of the most epic things to do! In Solo mode or with your mates, try stuff like the 'grey gun' only challenge or the 'one gun, one chest, no skydive' or the insanely tough 'no healing' challenge. Think of your own and stick to the rules.

TOP TIP
With your *Fortnite* friends, agree in advance on a date that you can all play and make up your own challenges together.

COMMUNITY

That means you, your friends, your squad members and the millions of *Fortnite* fans and players around the world! The *Fortnite* community is one of the strongest ever for an online game and every person who drops into the island wants it to be the best. You are not strictly in *Fortnite*, but you are the people who make *Fortnite* the force that it is!

FORTNITE FILE

THE MOST EPIC THING IN *FORTNITE* IS:

THE BEST SPECIAL THINGS ARE:

NEW WEAPONS: ☐   **NEW ITEMS:** ☐   **NEW COSMETICS:** ☐

NEW CHALLENGES: ☐

ON THE SCREEN BELOW, DRAW A POSTER TO HIGHLIGHT YOUR OWN SPECIAL EVENT, ITEM

OR CHALLENGE. ADD LABELS AND NAMES TO MAKE IT CRYSTAL CLEAR WHAT'S GOING ON.

TOP 10 ... SICK SAYINGS

Beginners and pros need to know the wicked words and sick sayings that players use in the game. Set your scopes on these top ten *Fortnite* phrases so that you understand exactly what your teammates mean!

1

GG

Players often use this phrase at the end of a match. It stands for 'good game' and is a compliment that's given when you want to praise a player. It's polite gaming to 'gg' your mates – leave without saying it and you could be accused of rage-quitting in *Fortnite*!

2

OP

You'll hear this being said and messaged all the time, especially if there's a devastating new weapon, vehicle or LTM. It means 'over-powered' and most Battle Royalers don't like an OP weapon because it unbalances gameplay and gives too much power to one player or team. For example, the infinity blade was seriously OP, dude!

TOP TIP
Epic Games listens to the *Fortnite* community. If you tell them and share with them that something is OP, they'll often react and look into it.

3 META

This might be a new *Fortnite* phrase for you, but it's handy when you're discussing team strategy. Meaning 'most effective tactic available', it's basically the best way that you can reach a Victory Royale. If there's a major update or new weapon that's dropped, the meta would be to make the most of this and outsmart the enemy. Always know what your meta is before leaving the bus!

4 ONE-SHOT

This can be used in a couple of shoot-out scenarios. A seriously monstrous weapon, like a heavy sniper rifle, has the ability to one-shot someone and eliminate them with a single bullet. It could also mean that an enemy has been hit a few times already and they are now 'one shot' – one more shot and they're finished!

TOP TIP
Even though it's good for your kill count, don't be too concerned about delivering the final shot that eliminates an enemy. If a teammate's in a better position to do so, let them fire the final shot.

5 NERFED

Perhaps as the result of a new gun or explosive being OP, an item can be nerfed by the makers. This results in having its damage or ability massively reduced. Battle Royale fans may not like this to start with, but most agree that things need nerfing now and then to level out the game.

TOP TIP
If you're old enough to have an account, keep up to date with Epic's nerfing by following their social channels or by checking the Epic website.

6 NO-SKIN

There's nothing wrong with being a no-skin, as all it means is a player wearing original skins and no fancy costumes. It doesn't impact on gameplay at all. It's a word that's also come to be used for someone who is a beginner and a bit of a 'noob' – a newcomer to *Fortnite*.

BUSH CAMPER

Pretty easy to work out this funny phrase, hey? If you're accused of being a bush camper, it means you're too nervous to come out of the bushes or the woods and take on the enemy. Hiding is all well and good and can be a solid tactic, but in *Fortnite* you've got to shoot and build to get the respect of your teammates and to progress in the game!

KNOCKED

You'll do well to survive a game without being knocked. Getting knocked means your health has been depleted and you could be eliminated if the enemy moves in on you while you're down. Similar to being 'lit up' and ripe for receiving a deadly strike.

9 90s

Doing '90s' is a building term that means you rapidly construct walls and ramps, in order to take the high ground in a gunfight. In each new section, you turn 90 degrees, lay two walls, a floor then a ramp, then turn again and carry on. It's a quick-fire phrase for a quick-fire technique that could save your bacon in a battle!

TOP TIP
To do 90s, try not to touch the walls as that will slow you down.

10 CHOKE

If you choke in *Fortnite*, then you mess things right up and lose from a winning position. Not a smart thing to do! For example, if you've got the high ground and a decent weapon, but still get eliminated by an inferior opponent, then you can rightly say that you choked on the battlefield. If you choke you're a joke, basically!

FORTNITE FILE

MY FAVOURITE *FORTNITE* PHRASE IS:

THREE NEW *FORTNITE* WORDS I'LL USE ARE:

1.

2.

3.

WRITE A QUICK 50-WORD BATTLE REPORT HERE. TRY TO USE AS MANY EPIC WORDS, SAYINGS AND PHRASES AS YOU CAN THINK OF. YOU CAN EVEN MAKE UP SOME NEW ONES AND TELL YOUR MATES WHAT THEY MEAN!

TOP 10 ... SKINS

Having a sick skin is such a big part of Battle Royale - especially when you combine it with some epic emote moves! There are hundreds in the game, but scan through this top 10 selection to see some of the best ever outfits and costumes and then design your own on page 63. Dress to impress, dudes!

1 SGT. WINTER

Dropping into *Fortnite* at Christmas, Sgt. Winter looks like a kickin' combo of Santa and a super-strong old dude! Don't worry about him getting a chill as he moves around the winter map without a jacket - this crusader is so hot in combat that he'll roast you up like a Christmas turkey!

2 SKULL TROOPER

First appearing at Halloween in 2017, and brought back for the spooky season each October, Skull Trooper is a classic Battle Royale outfit. The black and white suit is simple but very effective. It strikes fear into any squad, as no-one wants to take on a bone-crunching skeleton with a machine gun!

3 PEELY

Season 8's Battle Pass sprang a surprise with this fun, fruity *Fortnite* cosmetic! Peely is a funny outfit, but a little scary, too – a human banana surely belongs in the Fortnitemares LTM? It's definitely memorable, though, and gamers gave it a big thumbs up when it was released. Time to go bananas on the battlefield!

TOP TIP
Some skins really make you stand out on the map – a big, bright banana is easy to spot! You'll need to be extra stealthy in this gear.

4 SENTINEL

Described as a cross between a scary robotic chicken and a futuristic soldier, Sentinel's appearance in Season 9 caused quite a stir! Coming with the Battle Pass and as part of the Battle Dynamics set, it also features the Hot Wing back bling and Jump Jets emote as cool challenge rewards. It's not quite a rock-hard Iron Man vibe, but definitely one that's worth collecting and bringing into the battle! Squawk!

5 RAVAGE

Along with the Dark Wings back bling, Ravage is ready to rock *Fortnite*! Those glowing, haunting eyes and slim but powerful body shape make the wearer out to be a focused, ruthless and shadow-chasing assassin. Running into this skin in a Tilted Towers shoot-out is really not a good idea.

6 DANTE

Let's face it – you've got to be a Battle Royale hero if you can mix a skull with a rose on top of your head! And speaking of heads, Dante's petrifying party trick is that his make-up glows bright when the lights go out. That's surely enough to make you afraid of the dark!

TOP TIP
Dante is part of the Muertos set. This also features the Rosa skin, so you and your Duos buddy could perform the blingin' Best Mates emote like pros!

ROX

When this Legendary skin landed with the Season 9 Battle Pass, things got really colourful. With lots of options for customisation, such as multiple stages and secondary lighting colours you'll just have to make sure you don't stand out too much, especially if you go for the shocking pink!

FROSTBITE

We reckon this chilled-out gear is hugely underrated. It's a 'cool' blend of soldier, assassin, workman and, er, DJ that was available as part of the winter Deep Freeze Bundle. Team it up with the classic Dance Moves emote, pictured here, and your squad will think you're a retro fighter with some slick shooting skills!

9

CUDDLE TEAM LEADER

Released for Valentine's Day, you've got to be a bit wacky to fall in love with this Legendary costume! Pink, fluffy bears should be friendly and fun, but you definitely don't want to get too cosy with this character in combat. Cuddle Team Leader may look innocent, but the black broken heart design is a big clue to the pain it can cause!

10

DJ YONDER

Perhaps the perfect skin to bust out some epic emotes like Get Funky, Take The Elf and Floss! DJ Yonder is always in tune and is a mega mix of robot, llama and dangerous disco lights. Obviously not as daunting as the various knight skins in *Fortnite*, but the flashing disco pants will light up any midnight dance party!

FORTNITE FILE

MY FAVOURITE *FORTNITE* SKIN IS:

MY DEADLY DESIGN FOR MY OWN SKIN WOULD

LOOK LIKE ...

GOODBYE!

And that's it! It's been a blast counting down the 100 best bits ever with you. With so much awesome stuff in this game it was hard to keep it to 100 and we know you'll have your own favourite weapons, places and more that didn't make it into this book, but what we can agree on is that *Fortnite* is packed with great details, meaning that it's a game that's here to stay.

So throw yourself out of the Battle Bus and experience everything that's great about this game, from 1 to 100!

The 100% UNOFFICIAL *FORTNITE* TOP 100 team

SAFETY TIPS

YOUNGER FANS' GUIDE

Spending time online is great fun. As *Fortnite* might be your first experience of digital socialising, here are a few simple rules to help you stay safe and keep the internet an awesome place to spend time:
• Never give out your real name – don't use it as your username.
• Never give out any of your personal details.
• Never tell anybody which school you go to or how old you are.
• Never tell anybody your password, except a parent or guardian.
• Before registering with *Fortnite*, ask a parent or guardian for permission.
• Take regular breaks, as well as playing with parents nearby, or in shared family rooms.
• Always tell a parent or guardian if something is worrying you.

> **NOTE**
> *Fortnite: Battle Royale* is PEGI rated 12

PARENTS' GUIDE

ONLINE CHAT

In *Fortnite*, there is live, unmoderated voice and on-screen text chat between users. At the time of writing, turning off text chat isn't possible. You can, however, turn off voice chat:
• Open the Settings menu in the top right of the main *Fortnite* page, then the cog icon. Choose the Audio tab at the top of the screen. From there, you can adjust several audio features, including voice chat. Turn the setting from 'on' to 'off' by tapping the arrows.
• On consoles, you are also able to disable voice chat completely in the Parental Controls, or you can set it so your child can only chat with users who have previously been added as friends. It's important to stress to your child that they shouldn't add anyone as a friend they don't know in real life. To find these controls, see opposite about in-game purchases.

SOCIAL MEDIA SCAMS

There are many accounts on Facebook and Twitter that claim to give away free V-Bucks, which will be transferred to their account. Be sceptical – it's important to check the authenticity of these accounts and offers before giving away personal information.

SOUND

Fortnite is a game where sound is crucial. Players will often wear headphones, meaning parents won't be able to hear what is being said by strangers. Set up your console or computer to have sound coming from the TV as well as the headset so you can hear what other players are saying to your child.

REPORTING PLAYERS

If you see or hear a player being abusive, you can easily report them.
• Open the Settings menu in the main *Fortnite* page. Select the Feedback option, which allows you to report bugs, send comments or report players.
• After you've been eliminated from a game, you're also given an option to report a player by holding down the corresponding button at the bottom of the screen.

SCREEN TIME

Taking regular breaks is important. Set play sessions by using a timer. However, *Fortnite* games can last up to 20 minutes and if your child finishes playing in the middle of a round, they'll leave their teammates a person short and lose any points they've earned. So, it is advisable to give an advanced warning for stopping play.

IN-GAME PURCHASES

Fortnite does offer the ability to make in-game purchases such as new clothes, dances (emotes) and equipment, but they're not required to play the game. They also don't improve a player's performance.

To set up parental controls:
• For PlayStation 4, you can create special child accounts that can be linked to your adult account, which lets you set monthly spending limits. Log into your main PS4 account. Go to Settings > Parental Controls > Family Management. Choose Add Family Member > Create User, and then enter your child's name and date of birth. You can set up specific parental controls.

• For Xbox One, you can create a special passcode to verify purchases. Go to Settings > All Settings > Accounts > Sign-in. Then choose Change My Sign-In & Security Preferences, and scroll right to Customise. Scroll right again and select Ask For My Passkey To Make Purchases, and choose Passkey Required. Simply pick a PIN your child won't guess.

• For PC and Mac, go into the account settings of your child's Epic Games account. Once in there, make sure there aren't any card details or linked PayPal accounts. You can easily remove them if they are there.

• For iPhone and iPad, whenever you make a purchase, you'll always have to verify it with either a password, the Touch ID fingerprint scanner or Face ID. But some iPhones are set up so that you only have to enter a password every 15 minutes. To stop this, go to Settings > Your Name > iTunes & App Store. Underneath you'll see a Password Settings Section. Go to Purchases And In-App Purchases, and choose Always Require. If your child knows your iPhone password, you can set up a second PIN for purchases. Go to Settings > General > Restrictions, then press Enable Restrictions. Choose a new four-digit passcode for In-App Purchases.